A Guide for Using

Missing May

in the Classroom

Based on the novel written by Cynthia Rylant

*This guide written by **Janet Buckley** and **Lauren Corcoran***

Teacher Created Materials, Inc.
6421 Industry Way
Westminster, CA 92683
www.teachercreated.com
©2000 Teacher Created Materials, Inc.
Made in U.S.A.
ISBN 1-7439-3064-9

Edited by
Lorin Klistoff, M.A.

Illustrated by
Bruce Hedges

Cover Art by
Wendy Chang

Table of Contents

Introduction

Some books, through thought-provoking story lines and striking imagery, transport readers directly into the stories and are recognized for this artistry. They can stimulate our imaginations, inform our minds, inspire our higher selves, and fill our time with magic! With a good book, we are never lonely or bored. A good book only gets better with time because each reading brings us new meaning. Each new story is a treasure to cherish forever.

In Literature Units, we take great care to select books that will become treasured friends for life. The book *Missing May* by author Cynthia Rylant has received both the John Newbery Medal and the Boston Globe-Horn Book Award. The book is about what it means to be loved, losing someone dear, and learning to live with hope on the other side of bereavement. The author has written with honesty, sensitivity, and flashes of humor. Students everywhere are learning to love Summer, the main character, who wants to be a writer. They willingly climb aboard the story and travel the journey with her while she is learning about herself and missing May.

Teachers using this unit will find the following features to supplement their own valuable ideas.

- A Sample Lesson Plan
- Pre-reading Activities
- A Biographical Sketch and Picture of the Author
- A Book Summary
- Vocabulary Lists and Suggested Activities
- Journal Activities
- Chapters grouped for study, with each section including the following:

  —quizzes
  —hands-on projects
  —cooperative learning activities
  —cross-curriculum connections
  —extension activities to relate to the reader's own life

- Post-reading Activities
- Book Report Ideas
- Research Ideas
- Culminating Activities
- Three Different Options for Unit Tests
- Bibliography of Related Resources
- Answer Key

We are confident that this unit will be a valuable addition to your literature planning. Through the use of our ideas, your students will increase the circle of "friends" they have in books!

Sample Lesson Plan

Lesson 1
- Introduce and complete some of the pre-reading activities. (page 5)
- Read About the Author with your students. (page 6)
- Initiate an Into Your Life reading response journal. (page 16)

Lesson 2
- Introduce the vocabulary list for Section 1. (page 8)
- Read chapters 1–3. As you read, place the vocabulary words in the context of the story.
- Choose a vocabulary activity. (page 9)
- Make a bird feeder. (page 11)
- Complete Fears and Phobias. (page 12)
- Do Water Investigations. (pages 13 and 14)
- Complete Math in May's Cupboard. (page 15)
- Write in Personal Response Journal. (page 16)
- Administer Section 1 quiz. (page 10)

Lesson 3
- Introduce the vocabulary list for Section 2. (page 8)
- Read chapters 4 and 5. As you read, place the vocabulary words in the context of the story.
- Choose a vocabulary activity. (page 9)
- Create Surreal Art. (page 18)
- Complete the writing activity Pictures That Tell a Story. (page 19)
- Compare and contrast using a Venn diagram. (page 20)
- Write in Personal Response Journal. (page 16)
- Fill out the chart in Concrete Versus Abstract. (page 21)
- Administer Section 2 quiz. (page 17)

Lesson 4
- Introduce the vocabulary list for Section 3. (page 8)
- Read chapters 6 and 7. As you read, place the vocabulary words in the context of the story.
- Choose a vocabulary activity. (page 9)
- Create a Figurative Language Quilt. (page 23)
- Complete Small Medium at Large newspaper activity. (page 24)

- Learn about idioms. (page 25)
- Write in Personal Response Journal. (page 16)
- Answer the questions about Gifts. (page 26)
- Administer Section 3 quiz. (page 22)

Lesson 5
- Introduce the vocabulary list for Section 4. (page 8)
- Read chapters 8 and 9. As you read, place vocabulary words in the context of the story.
- Choose a vocabulary activity. (page 9)
- Create a Character Flip-Art Chart. (page 28)
- Do some online research and design a Charleston brochure. (pages 29 and 30)
- Use mapping skills for From Deep Water to Charleston Map. (page 31)
- Write in Personal Response Journal. (page 16)
- Complete Clues to Use. (page 32)
- Administer Section 4 quiz. (page 27)

Lesson 6
- Introduce vocabulary list for Section 5. (page 8)
- Read chapters 10–12. As you read, place vocabulary words in the context of the story.
- Choose a vocabulary activity. (page 9)
- Have a Hobby Fair. (page 34)
- Create a Newscast. (page 35)
- Write using Psychic Writing Prompts. (page 36)
- Write in Personal Response Journal. (page 16)
- Complete The Best Things in Life Are Free. (page 37)
- Administer Section 5 quiz. (page 33)

Lesson 7
- Have discussions and/or write about Any Questions? (page 38)
- Assign book reports. (page 39)
- Assign research reports. (page 40)
- Begin the following culminating activities: Tribute to May (page 41) and/or Whirligigs (page 42).

Lesson 8
- Administer Unit Tests 1, 2, and/or 3. (pages 43–45)
- Have a classroom celebration. (page 42)

Before the Book

Before you begin reading *Missing May* with your students, do some pre-reading activities to stimulate interest and enhance comprehension. The following activities may work well in your class. Feel free to extend these activities.

1. Predict what the story might be about just by hearing the title and looking at the cover illustration.

2. Tell students that the book is divided into two parts. The first part is called "Still as Night." Ask them to predict what that might mean. Brainstorm ideas to get them started. Ask them if there may be a connection between the title of the book and the title of Part I.

3. *Missing May* alludes to two stories with which students may be familiar: *Alice's Adventures in Wonderland* by Lewis Carroll and *The Wonderful Wizard of Oz* by Frank Baum. Review the plots of these stories through discussion or viewing of videos of the stories so students will have story details fresh in their minds as they read *Missing May*.

4. Find out if students have heard of Cynthia Rylant. Have they read the *Henry and Mudge* books, the Poppleton books, or other books she has written? What might they guess about the author from what they already know?

5. If you have a map of the continental United States, have students look for West Virginia, see what states are around it, and notice the topography of the state. The Appalachians play a large part in the history and settlement of West Virginia.

6. Read some picture books by Cynthia Rylant—like *Miss Maggie* and *When I Was Young in the Mountains*—with students to help them get a flavor for Appalachia and being poor in West Virginia.

7. There are many devices used in *Missing May* which make for good lessons along the way as the class is reading the book. Symbolism, strong characterization, flashbacks, vivid imagery, and idioms are used throughout the story. Even the division of *Missing May* into two parts shows a device used by the author to impart information. Provoke students to become aware of these devices and to wonder why an author might use them.

8. Have a class discussion about loss and how we, as a society, deal with our grief and with death. Perhaps students have lost family members, friends, or beloved pets. Students can discuss the ceremonies with which they are familiar and how they felt about the events.

9. Plant a classroom garden. The theme of gardening is very strong in *Missing May*. The garden can be planted indoors or outside, depending on space. If access to a garden patch is unavailable, students can grow things in cups or even in a child's swimming pool filled with dirt. Time of year will determine what seeds will grow in your area. Any local hardware store or garden shop will be able to offer suggestions for what to grow. If possible, plant a crop that can be harvested and eaten. When the book is complete, students can create whirligigs with hidden wishes. They can plant them in the garden and set their wishes free.

About the Author

Cynthia Rylant was born on June 6, 1954, in Hopewell, Virginia, to John Tune and Leatrel Rylant Smith. When she was young, her parents separated, and she went to live with her grandparents and cousins in a house in the Appalachian region of West Virginia. Her grandparents' house had no running water or electricity. It was this house which provided the spark of inspiration for Cynthia Rylant's first book, *When I Was Young in the Mountains*. Many of her other books are also set in West Virginia. Ms. Rylant remained with her grandparents while her mother attended nursing school. She greatly enjoyed playing pretend games like cops and robbers on bicycles, playing with dolls, drawing pictures, writing stories, and loving animals—especially cats and dogs.

When she was eight years old, Cynthia Rylant and her mother moved to the small, rural town of Beaver, West Virginia. They did not have a lot of money. The young Cynthia began to notice that they did not have as many material possessions as other people around them. In her book, *But I'll Be Back Again*, she said that as long as she stayed in Beaver, she felt she was somebody important, but as soon as she left Beaver to go anywhere else, her sense of being somebody special evaporated into nothing, and she became dull, ugly, and poor. She had not heard from her father for many years, but in her early teens, he contacted her. They planned to meet, but before this could happen, he died of illness. She has said this loss affected her deeply.

When it was time for college, Rylant attended Morris Harvey College (which is now the University of Charleston), receiving a Bachelor of Arts degree. She then attended Marshall University for a Master's degree in English and Kent State University to obtain a Master of Library Science degree in 1982. She worked as a college English professor and a children's librarian. She began reading books she had never had a chance to read before—children's books! Ms. Rylant said that reading children's books as an adult gave her a different perspective on writing books for children. Her many works include picture books like the Henry and Mudge series and the Poppleton series, volumes of poetry, her autobiography, short stories, and novels. Many of her books and stories have won writing awards. When asked about the themes of her stories, she once remarked that she gained a lot of personal gratification thinking of those people who didn't get any attention in the world and making them really valuable in her books.

Cynthia Rylant has been living with her son, Nate, her big dog, Martha Jane, her little dog, Leia, and her cats, Blueberry and Edward Velvetpaws, in Oregon.

(Information for this biography came from *Something About the Author*, Volume 7, pages 193–199. The Internet addresses are *http://www.tetranet.net/users/stolbert/research/rylant.html* and *http://www.simonsays.com*.)

Missing May

by Cynthia Rylant

(Orchard, 1992)

(Available in Canada, Gage Distributors; UK, Baker & Taylor International; AUS, Franklin Watts)

Missing May is set in Appalachia in the state of West Virginia. The book's protagonist is a twelve-year-old girl named Summer. Summer has been living with her loving elderly aunt and uncle, May and Ob, who adopted her when she was six. Prior to that, she had been passed from relative to relative in Ohio from the time her real mother had died.

May and Ob were poor. They lived in a trailer on a plot of land on the side of a mountain in a small town called Deep Water where they subsisted on a pension. May tended her garden, and Ob built whirligigs which he called "the mysteries."

As the book begins, Summer tells us that May has recently died. Summer is living with Ob, and both of them are struggling to maintain equilibrium after May's death. The formal funeral has not helped Summer and Ob deal with their grief. One day, they notice a seventh-grade boy, Cletus, who goes to school with Summer, poking around Ob's old Chevy sitting in the yard. Cletus claims to be looking for magazine pictures to add to his collection. It seems he wishes to deepen his acquaintance with Summer and befriend Ob. Summer is not interested in becoming friends with Cletus, but Ob enjoys his company. Cletus begins to spend more and more time at their home. Summer feels he is intruding, but he also seems to be better at cheering Ob up than she is. Ob wants to "communicate" with May, and since Cletus once had a near-death experience, he may be the perfect "afterlife antenna." They try to contact May in the garden, but nothing happens. After this, Ob says he feels incapable of caring for Summer. He acts unlike himself—not rising from bed in the morning, remaining in his pajamas all day. Summer becomes scared that she and Ob will lose each other.

Cletus saves the day. His collection of pictures and flyers and his great sense of timing start Summer and Ob on a journey to visit a Spiritualist church medium who talks with the dead. The trio heads off on a two-day trip to visit the Reverend Miriam B. Young to get some answers and to make a sightseeing trip to the capitol. They are doomed to disappointment when they reach the church and discover Reverend Young has died. Ob is stricken and herds the children toward home. Wrapped in his own despair, he bypasses the capitol on the way back to Deep Water. Cletus is clearly distressed and saddened not to see the capitol, and Summer is afraid for her future. Suddenly, Ob undergoes a transformation in the car and decides to care about the living. He makes a U-turn and takes Summer and Cletus to the capitol, cherishing his time with them. Upon arriving home in Deep Water, an owl flies over Summer, and she is strongly reminded of May. Her tears burst forth, and she grieves. Ob holds her tenderly as she cries. In the morning, they take Ob's whirligig "mysteries" out to May's garden, plant them, and the wind "sets everything free."

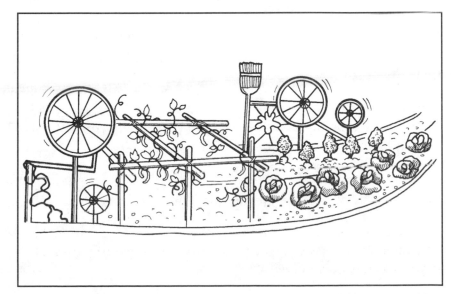

Vocabulary Lists

The vocabulary words listed below correspond to each section of *Missing May*. Ideas for vocabulary activities can be found on page 9 of this book.

Section 1 *(Chapters 1–3)*

recognize	lotion	thunk	cockeyed	grateful
hoisted	whirligigs	grunting	reliable	adrift
miraculously	jugs	stupefaction	revelations	fathom
fiddled	lunatic	vinyl	collaborate	solitary
genuinely	tweezing	delicate	constitution	speculations
enthralled	nudge	grin		

Section 2 *(Chapters 4–5)*

hovering	surreal	particular	suffragettes	bereavement
gaped	psychic	installing	lamely	puny
pitiful	enthusiasm	desperate	midst	optimism
ignorant	coveting	delirium	ailing	consoler
occasional	concrete	socialites	distorted	brilliant

Section 3 *(Chapters 6–7)*

infernal	trudged	vitally	silhouette	humiliated
stumped	brewing	exhilarated	ordinary	medium
glint	turnpike	philosophy	peg	hoax

Section 4 *(Chapters 8–9)*

hibernating	thawed	grubs	destined	adoration
astonishment	flabbergasted	deterioration	vulnerable	shrapnel
frail	exaggeration	johnnyhouse	fidgety	sprawled
majestic	elegant	artifacts	launched	serene

Section 5 *(Chapters 10–12)*

telepathically	imbecile	brazenly	feeble	traipsing
hobnobbing	tranquillity	kin	swooping	diabetes
spontaneously	combusting	oblivion	consolation	dumbfounded

8

Vocabulary Activity Ideas

You can help your students learn and retain the vocabulary in *Missing May* by providing them with interesting vocabulary activities. Here are a few ideas.

- ❏ **Cue Cards**—This is a partner activity. Using 20 vocabulary words per page, divide a page into two columns. In each of the columns, list ten different vocabulary words and their definitions. Fold the page lengthwise (blank-side in) and laminate it. Students sitting opposite each other can take turns quizzing their partners to match words with definitions.

- ❏ **Content Clues**—Before reading the chapters, find the sentence with the vocabulary word in it. Read the sentence to the students, leaving out the vocabulary word. Have students guess possible words before you reveal the word.

- ❏ **Mini Dictionary**—Make a small dictionary, using the vocabulary words. Alphabetize the words and write a definition for each one. The dictionary can be extended by including sentences showing word meaning, adding parts of speech, guide words, and illustrations.

- ❏ **Value of Words**—How much does each word cost? Consonants cost 1 cent, vowels cost 25 cents, and syllables cost $1.00. Which word is the most expensive? least expensive?

- ❏ **Vocabulary Game Boards**—Divide students into groups of three or four. Give each group a large piece of paper or cardboard on which to create their game. Assign each group a section of the vocabulary words from the book. Each group should design a game board, create rules, and make clues for the vocabulary words on their list. Ideas for clue cards may include riddles, sentences with words left out, or scrambled letters.

- ❏ **Baseball Spelling**—Divide the class into two teams. Designate first, second, third, and home bases around the classroom. If the player up to bat (spelling the word) spells it correctly, he or she moves to first base. The team with the most runs wins the game.

- ❏ **Categorize**—Categorize words into five groups: nouns, verbs, adjectives, adverbs, or other.

- ❏ **Silent Match-Up**—Make two sets of cards. Each set has vocabulary word cards and definition cards. Divide the class into two teams. Each player takes a turn matching one definition at a time. If one player sees a wrong match, he or she can correct it. The team with the most correct matches wins.

- ❏ **Beanbag Toss**—The student in possession of the beanbag takes a turn using one of the vocabulary words in a sentence. Afterward, he or she tosses the beanbag to another student who then chooses another vocabulary word and makes a new sentence. This continues until all the words are used or all students have had the opportunity to make a sentence.

- ❏ **Go Fish**—Create a deck containing vocabulary word cards and definition cards. In groups of four, players are dealt five cards and play "Go Fish," matching words with their definitions to form a "book." The player with the most "books" wins.

- ❏ **Mixed-up Words Game**—Have student teams scramble vocabulary words for other student teams to unscramble.

- ❏ **Vocabulary Stories**—Have two to four students in a group write on any subject and include at least ten words from the vocabulary words listed on page 8.

Quiz Time

Answer the following questions about Chapters 1–3. If you need more writing space, use the back of this paper or a separate piece of paper.

1. Who were Summer, May, and Ob?

   _____

   _____

2. Where and with whom did Summer live before coming to live with May and Ob?

   _____

   _____

3. Why did May and Ob bring Summer home with them?

   _____

   _____

4. What were some ways May and Ob showed their love for Summer when they first brought her home?

   _____

   _____

5. How did May feel when they would pack to go visit relatives in Ohio?

   _____

   _____

6. Did Summer believe May's spirit had visited Ob?

   _____

   _____

7. How did Summer and Ob keep their minds off May?

   _____

   _____

8. Why did May have a hopeless kind of fear about water?

   _____

   _____

9. Who was Cletus, and how does he know Summer?

   _____

   _____

10. On the back of this paper, answer the following question: Explain what Summer means when she says that after all those years of having nobody, having Ob and May was her idea of dying and going to heaven.

Making a Bird Feeder

In Chapter 2, Ob and Summer are outside cutting open milk jugs to make into bird feeders. The characters in this book care about nature and the creatures around them. Making bird feeders out of recycled milk cartons is good for the earth and good for your local birds. The bird feeders can be hung around the school grounds, hung outside the classroom, or students can take them home to hang.

Materials

- recycled pint-size milk carton for each student
- two twigs at least 2" to 3" (5 cm to 8 cm) long for each student
- scissors
- heavy yarn or string
- construction paper
- glue or tape
- colored markers
- bird seed

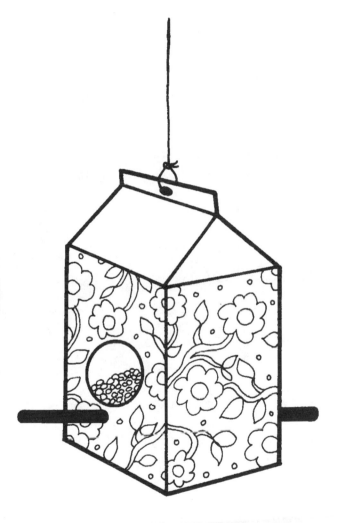

Directions

1. Have students bring in washed milk cartons and twigs. (Extras may be obtained from the school lunchroom.) Make certain all milk cartons are clean and dry.

2. Cut a 2" (5 cm) diameter hole on opposite sides of the milk carton, halfway up the side.

3. Below the 2" (5 cm) holes, poke smaller holes for the perch (an easy way to do this is to cut a small x through which a stick or the perch will be able to poke).

4. Cut a small hole in the center of the top of the carton to hang the bird feeder.

5. Push the twigs in the small holes on each side. These are the perches.

6. If you choose, you can decorate the feeder with colored paper and designs. If glue is used, let bird feeders dry a few hours before filling them with seed.

7. Tie a 2' (61 cm) length of heavy yarn or string through the center hole.

8. Fill the bird feeder with seeds and hang it.

Fears and Phobias

May had fears or phobias which are revealed in Chapter 2. She was afraid to visit her relatives in Ohio because she worried something would happen to her home while she was gone. She was also afraid of water since she had lost her parents in a flood.

Most people have a fear or phobia of something. Sometimes people know why they are afraid of something—like May with the water. Other times, people do not know what causes their phobias. Some people are afraid of spiders. Others are afraid of heights. Many people are ashamed of their fears. They keep them a secret, but everyone has fears and they are nothing to be ashamed of. Sometimes your fears can lessen or go away when you learn more about them.

Directions

1. Divide the class into small groups.
2. Give each group one of the following phobias to work on together.
   - fear of heights
   - fear of spiders
   - fear of water
   - fear of speaking in front of the class
   - fear of dogs
   - fear of storms
   - fear of fire
   - fear of the wilderness
   - fear of the dark
   - fear of amusement park rides
   - fear of rats
   - fear of snakes
   - fear of being abandoned

3. Groups should answer the following questions together, giving each member a chance to respond to each question.
   - What might cause someone to have this fear?
   - Are there ways in which this fear might help someone? (For example, a fear of fire could keep someone away from fires and lessen their chance of getting burned.)
   - Without doing anything dangerous, what are some ways someone might learn about this fear?
   - How could someone get help with this fear?
   - What could someone with this fear do to overcome or control the fear?
4. When groups have answered the questions, each group presents their fear and fear strategies to the class.

Extension

A cross-curricular connection that is fun is to graph students' fears without revealing names. The teacher can make a fear survey. (Do not include highly personal or sensitive fears which would reveal student identity.) This helps students to see that if they have a particular fear, there may be others in the class who may have the same or similar fears or phobias. Use the data from the fear surveys to create a class graph. Students can write and answer math word problems based on chart data. They can also research the most common phobias—facts can sometimes lessen fear.

Water Investigations

May's mother and father were killed in a flash flood when May was nine years old, but May survived. Her mother heard the floodwaters and rushed to put May in a metal washtub. During the flood, May floated six miles away from her home in the tub and was rescued there with a kitten she had saved from the waters.

Brainstorm: Why do some things float but others sink?_____

_____

Experiment 1: Which objects will float, and which will sink?

Materials: large container (small aquarium), water, variety of objects (wooden block, piece of metal, piece of aluminum foil, small ball, cup, marble, funnel, etc.)

Activity: Choose one object at a time and predict whether it will float or sink. Record the results on the chart below.

Object	Prediction		Results		Possible Reason
	Sink	Float	Sink	Float	

Conclusion: _____

_____

Water Investigations (cont.)

Experiment 2: Which shape floats the best?

Materials: four different colors of clay, one large container of water, scale, clock

Activity: Make sure all pieces of clay weigh the same amount. Mold each into a different shape that you think will float, including one with a hull shape. Place each one in the water for one minute and record which shapes remain floating for that time.

Shape	Sinks	Floats	Time

Conclusion: _____

_____

1. What makes it possible for a raft to float? _____
2. Why are boats hull-shaped?_____

(*Note:* About 250 B.C., the scientist Archimedes discovered the Law of Buoyancy. It states that the force on a submerged object is equal to the water it displaces.)

Experiment 3: What does density have to do with floating and sinking? Will ice float in other liquids as it does in water?

Materials: two glasses, water, isopropyl alcohol, two ice cubes the same size

Activity: Pour water in one glass, leaving some room for ice. Pour an equal amount of isopropyl alcohol in the other glass. Now, place an ice cube in each. What do you notice?

_____

Why?_____

(*Note:* An Internet site to visit is *http://www.pbs.org/wgbh/nova/lasalle/buoypool.html*, which is NOVA Online. Students interested in displacement and buoyancy might want to see the Boat-in-Pool Puzzler 2. This puzzler shows a boat in a pool. The question is whether a rock displaces more water in the pool if it is in the boat or just in the water. Students can formulate theories and check answers.)

Math in May's Cupboard

Summer was delighted with the food in May and Ob's kitchen cupboard. She saw Oreos®, Ruffles®, and Snickers®. There were little cardboard boxes of juice, fat bags of marshmallows, cans of SpaghettiOs®, and a little plastic bear full of honey. There were glass bottles of Coke® in the refrigerator and a large half of a watermelon. The best item May saw was a carton of Hershey's® real chocolate milk. (Chapter 1)

Cupboard   **Refrigerator**

Directions: Please answer the following questions. Use the margins, the back of this paper, or a separate scrap of paper to work out the problems.

1. If all the items shown above were bought at one time, how much would they cost?

   _____

2. How much would one can of SpaghettiOs cost? _____ one Snickers bar? _____ two boxes of juice? _____

3. If you had a $20 bill and bought a bag of Ruffles and one bottle of Coke, how much change would you receive? _____

4. At the store, suppose there is a special ¹/₂-off sale on Snickers bars. How much would it cost you to buy 36 of these? _____ Explain how you know this. _____

   _____

5. Ellet's store sells three boxes of juice for $1.80. The same juice is sold at the supermarket for $0.70 a box. Which store has the better buy? _____

6. There is a one-day special on cookies: buy one, get one free. If you only had five dollars, could you afford to buy four bags? _____

7. The price of watermelon went up to $0.17 per pound. If you were to buy another 19-pound watermelon, what would be the difference in price? _____

8. From the prices above, what costs exactly 4 quarters, 15 dimes, 9 nickels, and 4 pennies?

   _____

Personal Response Journal

Missing May is a personal book, evoking thoughts and feelings on the nature and meaning of family, friendship, overcoming tragedy, and healing. The book is written from Summer's point of view, and we almost feel as if we are reading her personal journal as we read along in the book. Journal writing is a terrific way to help students connect with the ideas and with the characters. The book itself can be used as an example to guide students in this activity. To encourage student interest in writing, a selection of topics for journal responses is provided below.

Guidelines and Suggestions

Journals can be made with 12" x 18" (30 cm x 46 cm) construction paper folded in half (for the folder) with loose, lined paper placed inside for student journal entries. When the book is completed, the pages can be stapled together for a permanent keepsake.

Tell the students that the journals are for them to record their thoughts and ideas about the reading, about their own personal experiences they may be reminded of as they read, and about any questions they might have as they read. Journals are best kept as private communications between student and teacher unless an opportunity arises when a student volunteers to read a response aloud. Give students time to write in their journals several times a week. Journals should not be corrected or assigned letter grades but should reflect adequate attention to the questions.

Good ideas for journal responses include the following:

- Cynthia Rylant alludes to *Alice's Adventures in Wonderland* and to *The Wonderful Wizard of Oz* in several places throughout the book. Students can write about these references. (For example, Summer feels she has fallen into Wonderland because she can't believe May and Ob have brought her home. She is enchanted by the whirligigs Ob creates and thrilled by the food selections in May's cupboard. Let students tell why they think this feels like Wonderland to Summer. Then, have them write what Wonderland would feel like to them.)

- Describe each of the four characters in the book, one at a time. How do you feel about each? What has this character done, or what characteristics does this character have, that cause you to feel this way?

- Discuss the whole idea of family presented throughout the book. What is Summer's idea of family? What are your ideas of family? Beyond providing someone with shelter, food, drink, and clothing, what makes a good family?

- Discuss Summer's relationship with Cletus and how it changes. Why do you think it changes? Has your relationship with a friend or family member changed over time? How has it changed? What may have caused it to change? Are you happy with the change?

- For what are the characters in the book searching or looking? What do they seem to need? Ask students to write about what they think their own needs and hopes are.

Quiz Time

Answer the following questions about Chapters 4 and 5. If you need more writing space, use the back of this paper or a separate piece of paper.

1. What did Cletus collect in his suitcase? Why did he like them?

   _____

   _____

2. Where did Cletus get the things he collected?

   _____

   _____

3. How did Cletus describe *surreal*?

   _____

   _____

4. What did Ob do differently in the morning that had Summer worried?

   _____

   _____

5. Restate the near-death experience Cletus had when he was younger.

   _____

   _____

6. Who was the person Summer refers to as the "afterlife antenna"? Why was this person called this?

   _____

   _____

7. Why did Ob take Summer and Cletus out into May's garden?

   _____

   _____

8. What did Ob say when he talked about May in the garden?

   _____

   _____

9. About what was Ob disappointed when he left Summer and Cletus in the garden? Was Summer disappointed too?

   _____

   _____

10. On the back of this paper, please give Summer's reasons why the traditional funeral did not help them recover from their grief.

Surreal Art

Cletus showed Summer an old photograph. He described surreal art as taking something real and stretching it out into a thing that's true but distorted.

Surrealism is a modern form of art that was founded in the 1920s. Many surrealists create art that makes viewers want to take a double look. Objects or subjects seem to be real but also appear in a way that is beyond real—as in a dream. It is art that is fact but fantasy, awake but dreamlike, logical but illogical.

One famous artist, Salvador Dali, created an interesting painting in which he fused a fish on a goblet. Salvador Dali's painting *The Persistence of Memory* (1931) ranks as one of the most famous paintings of the 20th century. A surrealist, Dali referred to his work as "hand-painted dream photographs" and claimed that his imagery often came directly from his own dreams.

James Seaboar painted another interesting painting which features an aquarium full of fish with human faces. Other dreamlike ideas surreal artists have used include the following: trees with birds in place of leaves, older people dressed like young teenagers, and a face peeled like an apple peel.

Materials

- white construction paper
- pencils
- color medium (paint, markers, or crayons)

Directions

1. Have students close their eyes and think of something they wish they could do. For example, "If you wish you could fly, see your arms turn to wings. If you wish you could swim as smoothly as a fish, see your legs become a large fin. If you like to paint, imagine your arms become big brushes full of color."

2. Tell students to begin with real objects in their minds. Tell them to think of a way to put these objects together in a way that is beyond real—maybe even weird. Some possible examples include tigers with red and purple stripes, Dalmation dogs black with white spots, or people playing with a square baseball.

3. Tell them to put their creations on paper and give them titles.

Extension

Make the classroom an art museum. When the artwork is complete, display it on classroom walls. Invite other classes into your museum.

Pictures That Tell a Story

Cletus looked through magazines and peoples' photographs as if he were sampling a box of chocolates (Chapter 4). He had a great imagination and liked to create stories about the pictures he collected.

Before the Lesson

Have students bring in old magazines that contain photos of people. The teacher should cut out photos of people of different backgrounds in interesting settings doing a variety of activities.

Directions

1. Hand out a different picture to each student.

2. Have each student write a story about the person in the picture. If you want to use prompts to help them write, some suggestions are given below.

   - What is this person's name?
   - What is the person doing? Why?
   - Where does this person live?
   - What does this person do for a living?
   - Does he or she like his or her job? Why or why not?
   - Where and when did you meet this person?
   - Tell us one thing you learned from this person.
   - What event is coming soon?
   - How does he or she feel about it? Why?
   - What do you hope or wish for this person?

3. After students have written their stories, move them into groups of four and instruct them to take turns sharing their stories.

Extensions

- *Group Story*—The students write a group story connecting all their characters. Groups take turns reading their group stories to the class.

- *Computer Stories*—If computers or a computer lab are available, students can practice keyboard skills by typing these stories out to be displayed on the wall with the pictures.

- *Round-Robin Stories*—Stories can be created by groups. Place students into groups of four. Pass out one picture per group. Ask students to work without talking. The teacher reads the first prompt and Student 1 answers. Then he or she silently passes the paper to Student 2. Student 2 answers the second prompt and silently passes the paper to Student 3. This continues until all prompts are answered. Then the students work together to write a cohesive story from the answers they have provided. These prompts will help make the story interesting, reflect attributes of the picture, and help the story make sense.

- *Writer's Circle*—When the students finish their stories and read them aloud, have them critique the stories by asking the following questions: What did they like about the story? What were their concerns as a reader or listener? Do they have any other questions or suggestions?

Compare and Contrast

There were two ceremonies that marked the passing of May. One was the traditional ceremony, which was the funeral, and the other took place in the garden as described in Chapter 5.

Compare and contrast the two ceremonies by filling in the Venn diagram. Place May's funeral details in one circle and the characteristics of the ceremony in the garden in the other circle. Details that the two events have in common go in the overlapped area. Use your book if you need more details.

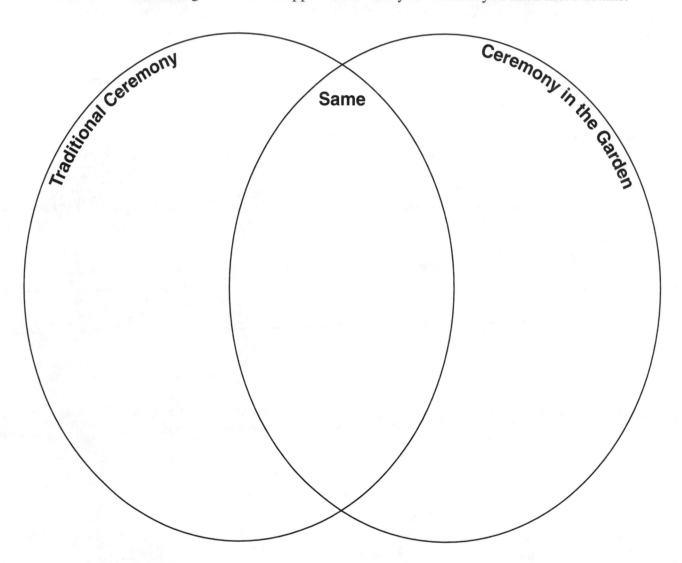

Answer the questions below.

1. Which funeral was more healing for Summer and Ob? Why? _____

   _____

   _____

2. Why do we have organized funerals? _____

   _____

   _____

Concrete Versus Abstract

Cletus said that Ob's whirligigs were not made from something we can understand. He commented that Ob didn't carve out little dogs and kittens because he didn't care about concrete things. Ob's "mysteries" were about abstract ideas.

Ob is tall, skinny, and older. These are all concrete facts about Ob—things we can use one or all of our five senses to detect. An abstract thing about Ob is his sense of humor. You can tell he has one when he tells a joke or laughs at a joke, but a sense of humor is an idea—you can not see or feel it. Something concrete about Cletus is his greasy hair. Something abstract is his love of things that are surreal.

Directions: Let's find out your concrete and your abstract features. Fill out the chart below with ten concrete and ten abstract facts about yourself.

Name _____

Concrete	Abstract
1. _____	1. _____
2. _____	2. _____
3. _____	3. _____
4. _____	4. _____
5. _____	5. _____
6. _____	6. _____
7. _____	7. _____
8. _____	8. _____
9. _____	9. _____
10. _____	10. _____

Quiz Time

Answer the following questions about Chapters 6 and 7. If you need more writing space, use the back of this paper or a separate piece of paper.

1. Summer said that guidance comes to her in the form of a greasy-haired lunatic. What did she mean?

   _____

   _____

2. Summer was afraid because Ob had changed when May did not appear. How did Ob change?

   _____

   _____

3. When Summer was in fourth grade, her teacher made her class write descriptions of each other. What words did Summer's classmates use to describe her?

   _____

   _____

4. Why didn't Summer realize her classmates were describing her?

   _____

   _____

5. Ob said, "Summer, I don't know that I can do it." What did Ob mean?

   _____

   _____

6. Why couldn't Ob begin work on a new whirligig?

   _____

   _____

7. What was hidden in Cletus' suitcase that gave him a way to help Ob?

   _____

   _____

8. Explain what Summer meant when she said that she "passed the torch" to Cletus.

   _____

   _____

9. What was a "Renaissance man," and what did it have to do with Cletus?

   _____

   _____

10. On the back of this paper, please answer the following questions: What did Summer mean when she said their journey was like taking directions to Oz? How do Summer and Ob feel differently about the trip to Putnam County?

Figurative Language Quilt

Cynthia Rylant's figurative language adds flavor and excitement to her writing. For example, she describes Mrs. Underwood as looking like dried-out apples.

A beautiful paper quilt can be created by the students as they learn to recognize similes, metaphors, and descriptive language.

Materials

- 5" x 7" (13 cm x 18 cm) index cards, preferably without lines
- pencils
- crayons or colored markers

Directions

1. Discuss with the class the types of figurative language found in *Missing May*. The most common forms are the following:
   - **simile**—a comparison of unlike things using the words *like* or *as* (Example: "He was as strong as a bull.")
   - **metaphor**—a comparison of unlike things when one object becomes another, using the word *is* (Example: "He is a tower of strength.")
   - **descriptive language**—using words to create a mental image (Example: "This muscle-bound, power-house of a man lifted tons of steel.")

2. Working with partners, students will look for examples of figurative language in sections 1, 2, and 3 of the book. Starting with Chapters 1–3, students find their favorite examples of similes, metaphors, or enriched, descriptive language. They write these down on lined paper or use scraps of paper to mark the pages. They do the same for Chapters 4–7.

3. Next, partner groups take turns reading their selections to the class. This way, the quilt squares will not be duplicated.

4. When done with their presentations, partners copy their three sentences onto three large index cards. For each card they must label the type of figurative language represented, list the page number, and decorate the card.

5. Collect all cards and make a class paper quilt to display on your wall.

Small Medium at Large

Cletus clipped a picture of the Spiritualist church leader, Reverend Young, out of the newspaper. The title of the article read: "The Reverend Miriam B. Young: Small Medium at Large." Cletus said that he would love to write newspaper titles when he grows up.

Newspaper titles summarize the articles that follow. They are designed to catch people's eyes and make them interested enough to read the article. Sometimes, it is possible to use a pun (play on words) such as the title "Small Medium at Large." Use the following newspaper activities to help students develop writing skills.

Create a News Story

Have the students read the following three newspaper article titles and write a few sentences telling about the news story: "Seeing Stars," "Seeing Red," and "Bark Is Worse Than Bite." (*Note:* Possible answers to these three are in the Answer Key.)

Summarize the Story

Read the following news story. When you have finished, have students summarize the main idea of the article, keeping in mind the answer to "who, what, when, where, why, and how" questions.

> Tangled Trails, Co.—A footrace scheduled to begin today through 40 miles of the Rocky Mountain region of Colorado called Tangled Trails has been rescheduled to begin next week due to a fierce hailstorm moving down from Canada. Participants expressed regret about the delay but rushed to find cover in local motels as the storm broke out, bombarding attendees with hard balls of ice. One would-be race entrant was knocked out by a large lump of hail and was taken to Mercury Mountain Hospital in the nearby town of Small Rock. She is reported in good condition and is expected to be released later today.

Pair students in partners. Using the summary as a starting place, have them create one or more titles for the article above. Think about whether there is an appropriate pun and about what would catch a reader's eye.

In a class discussion after this exercise, student partners share their titles with the class and justify the logic of their titles. The class can vote on the best title.

Create Titles for Articles

Pass out real newspaper articles to students with titles cut off (save titles). Students read the articles and create new titles that reflect the contents of the articles. See if they can match the original newspaper titles to the articles for which they created their own titles. Have students compare their own titles to the original titles. Ask them to look for the subjects and predicates and also see how the titles summarize the articles and catch the readers' eyes, making them want to read on.

Idioms

An idiom is a group of words that make up a phrase that has a special meaning different from what the words would ordinarily mean. The author of *Missing May* uses idioms often to create a sense of informality and add imagery to the story. For example, in Chapter 4, Ob and Summer had their eyes "glued on" Cletus. In this example, Summer and Ob do not use real glue on their eyes. It is an idiom which means they were watching Cletus carefully.

Match the Idioms

Read each idiom and find the correct meaning by placing the letter on the line.

1. _____ You're in the doghouse.   A. tricked me

2. _____ She's a cold fish.   B. is a pest

3. _____ My little sister gets in my hair.   C. feeling crazy

4. _____ My granddaughter pulled the wool over my eyes.   D. couldn't keep a secret

5. _____ It's raining cats and dogs.   E. unfriendly

6. _____ He spilled the beans.   F. in trouble

7. _____ I'm going batty.   G. heavily

Search for Idioms

Look in Chapters 6 and 7. Find three examples of idioms, write them down below (be sure to mark the page numbers), and write what you think they mean.

8. _____

9. _____

10. _____

Define Idioms

See if you can figure out the meanings of the following idioms. Write down your best guess for each idiom. When you are through, the class can find out the real meanings.

11. break the ice _____

12. don't change horses mid-stream _____

13. fish out of water _____

14. water under the bridge _____

15. walk on water _____

16. wet behind the cars _____

17. in hot water _____

18. babbling brook _____

19. not the only fish in the sea _____

20. looks like a drowned rat _____

21. mouth-watering _____

22. water rolling off a duck's back _____

Gifts

On the day that Ob did not get out of bed and Summer stayed home from school, Cletus visited them after school. Summer commented that Cletus never once asked why she was not at school that day. She also mentioned that he never once commented on Ob being in his pajamas. Summer noticed that Cletus had some gifts and that May would have said that he was "full of wonders," just like Ob. She thought that May would have liked him because she thought May always liked the unusual ones the best.

We usually think of gifts as presents someone gives you for your birthday or at other celebrations. The kind of gift Summer means does not cost anything. The gift Summer meant was a natural talent or ability.

Directions: In the spaces below, please answer the following questions.

1. What was the talent Summer says Cletus has?

   _____

   _____

2. How could Cletus' talent help people?

   _____

   _____

3. Did Summer have any gifts?

   _____

   _____

4. What were Ob's gifts?

   _____

   _____

5. What was May's gift?

   _____

   _____

6. What do you think your gifts are?

   _____

   _____

7. Do any of your gifts help people? In what ways do they help?

   _____

   _____

8. Is there a person whose gifts you admire? How do you think the person got those gifts?

   _____

   _____

9. What gifts would you like to have?

   _____

   _____

10. Is there a way to increase your talents/gifts?

   _____

   _____

Quiz Time

Answer the following questions about Chapters 8 and 9. If you need more writing space, use the back of this paper or a separate piece of paper.

1. What creatures used to get into the trailer?_____

_____

2. How did these creatures wake up Summer? _____

_____

3. How did May accidentally injure one of these creatures? How did she try to save it?

_____

_____

4. How did the creatures get into the trailer? _____

_____

5. What did Ob do to prevent more creatures from entering the trailer? _____

_____

6. What was the real purpose of the trip to Charleston? _____

_____

7. Why didn't Cletus and Ob tell the Underwoods the real purpose of the trip? _____

_____

8. The three people have their own reasons for the trip. What was Ob's reason? Summer's? Cletus'?

_____

_____

_____

9. At 3:25, Cletus Underwood and his suitcase showed up at the door, and they finally got directions to "Oz." What were the directions?

_____

_____

_____

10. On the back of this paper, write your prediction of what you think is going to happen in the story. Justify your reasons.

Character Flip-Art Chart

Aside from the cover of *Missing May*, the book has no pictures of the characters. All of our ideas about Summer, May, Ob, and Cletus come from images created from clues in the writing. This fun activity will show you what details your students can recall and will let you see how your students imagine the characters look.

Materials

- 9" x 12" (23 cm x 30 cm) construction paper for each student
- scissors
- crayons or markers

Directions

1. As you give the folding directions to your students, demonstrate each step to them. First, fold construction paper lengthwise (hotdog style). Crease the fold. Open up the paper.

2. Next, fold the paper widthwise (hamburger style). Fold again. Open up the paper. You should have eight equal rectangles.

3. Close the paper lengthwise, with the open end toward you. Now, draw and label a picture of each character in each of the four rectangles on top. Cut along the folded lines to the center fold between each character. Now each character is on a separate flap. Open each flap and write a description of each character, using as many details as possible.

1.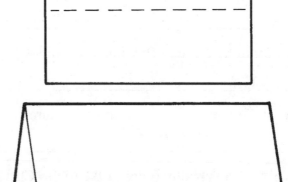

2.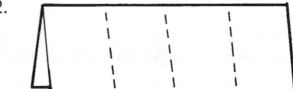

3.

Making a Charleston Brochure

Cletus became excited as he saw the state capitol. He thought about all the important people making laws under the gold dome.

Materials (per group)

- 1 #10 envelope and stamp
- notepaper
- colored pencils, crayons, or markers
- piece of 9" x 12" (23 cm x 30 cm) white paper
- pencils

General Directions

1. In groups of four, have students conduct online research about Charleston, the capital of West Virginia. (See Internet Research Directions on page 30.)

2. Have students incorporate the facts they learn into colorful, informative, well-written brochures. (*Note:* If your students do not have Internet access, you can write to the Charleston Convention and Visitors Bureau at 200 Civic Center Drive, Charleston, WV 25301, and request their visitor's packet.)

3. Tell students that the brochures must include at least three facts about each of the following subjects:

   - the state capitol (including a picture)
   - landmarks
   - sightseeing
   - culture and arts
   - recreation

4. The brochure will be on white paper folded (letter fashion) in thirds. On the front is the title. A picture of the state capitol and three facts about it, three facts about landmarks, and three facts about sightseeing are on the inside of the brochure. On the inside flap are culture and arts facts, and on the back, recreation. (See illustration below.)

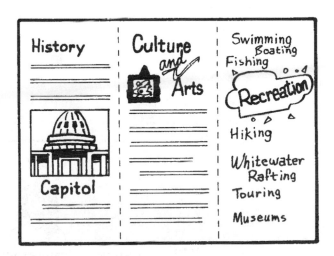

Making a Charleston Brochure *(cont.)*

Internet Research Directions

1. Log on to the computer and enter the following Internet address: *http://charlestonwv.com*.

2. The U. S. P. S. mailing address for the Charleston Convention and Visitors Bureau is on the home page. Students should write this address on their #10 envelope, as well as their return address. They must write a note asking for a brochure about Charleston to be sent to them. Later, students will be able to compare their brochures with the "official" one.

3. A sidebar to the home page has hyperlinks which are underlined. Click on The City.

4. This page offers three choices: Area History, Culture & Arts, and Recreation. Click on Area History. A page appears which has hyperlinks to The Capitol, Landmarks, and Sight-Seeing and Attractions. Print this page to get a picture of the capitol, or use colored pencils or crayons to draw a sketch of the capitol from the colored picture on the screen. The picture drawn should be able to fit into the brochure.

5. Next, have students click on The Capitol. Have them find their three major facts about the state capitol and supporting details. When finished, click on the Back arrow button.

6. Click on Landmarks. Have students find out at least three important landmarks and what is interesting about them. When finished, click on the Back arrow button. Now, do the same for Sight-Seeing and Attractions.

7. Click on the Back arrow button until the students are back at the page which says "The City" at the top. Click on the Culture & Arts and Recreation hyperlinks to get at least three facts and details from each. Finally, click on the Home button on the toolbar to go home.

8. Using complete sentences, persuasive language, and pictures, groups create their brochures. When all groups have completed the project, have group presentations. Then, put their work on display! When the "real" brochures arrive in the mail, compare them to the class versions for fun.

(*Note:* Be sure to access the Web site before engaging students in the activity. Web sites tend to change over time. If for some reason the Web site listed is no longer available, try one of the alternate URLs. Also, follow your school's policy about students' use of the Internet. Parental consent or close adult supervision of students' use of the Internet may be needed.)

From Deep Water to Charleston Map

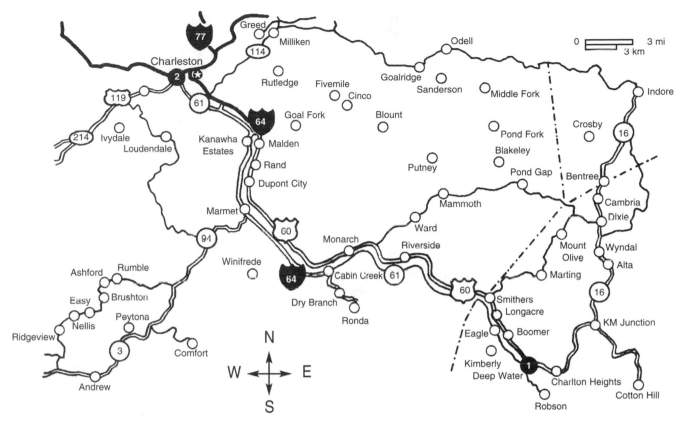

From: Deep Water, WV   Total Distance: 34.23 miles (54.77 km)
To: Charleston, WV   Estimated Time: 1 hr. 1 minute

1. Look at the scale at the top right-hand corner of the map. Use your ruler to measure and record the 3 mi. (3 miles) scale. _____ = 3 mi. Now measure kilometers. _____ = 3 km

2. How many inches equal 24 miles? _____ How many centimeters equal 24 kilometers? _____

3. 30 mi. = _____ inches 30 km = _____ centimeters

4. Which city, Charleston or Deep Water, is farther north? _____

5. What direction is Deep Water from Charleston? _____

6. As the crow flies (if a bird were flying in a straight line), the distance between Charleston and Deep Water is 25 miles or 40 kilometers. How many extra miles are added because of the curves in the roads? _____ How many extra kilometers? _____

7. How many miles is it to drive round trip? _____ How many kilometers? _____

8. Which main highways do you use? _____

9. If you wanted to take a rest approximately halfway to your destination, where would you stop? _____ How many miles/kilometers is it from Deep Water? _____ How many miles/kilometers do you have left to travel? _____

10. Write out directions from Deep Water to Charleston. (Write your answer on the back of this paper.)

Clues to Use

Summer felt she learned a lot about Cletus when she and Ob visited his home. She learned the following facts: (1) Cletus' house was tiny and brown, not much bigger than some people's garages. (2) The house sat far back from the road in a clump of pines. Summer knew in an instant that this was not the same boy who had been coming to her home with his battered old suitcase.

Clues in *Missing May*

Directions: Answer the following questions in the space below.

1. What did Summer learn about Cletus? (What was his home like inside? What were his parents like? What things did they keep in their house?)

   _____

   _____

   _____

2. Could Summer tell what Cletus' family valued by what they displayed in their house? Review the pages of Summer's visit to Cletus' house for details, if necessary.

   _____

   _____

   _____

3. How do you think Summer's feelings change toward Cletus from the visit? Is there evidence in the book to show a definite change?

   _____

   _____

Clues About You

4. What would someone learn about you by visiting your room or house? (Would they be able to see what colors you like? Could they see what your interests are? Would they be able to see who lives with you? Would they learn other interesting things, like whether you have pets?)

   _____

   _____

   _____

5. Which details might give them the most information about you?

   _____

   _____

6. Have you ever learned more about one of your friends after visiting his/her house?

   _____

Quiz Time

Answer the following questions about Chapters 10–12. If you need more writing space, use the back of this paper or a separate piece of paper.

1. What was the unexpected news Ob was told when he got to the Spiritualist church?

   _____

   _____

2. The unexpected news made a change in their plans. What did Ob decide to do?

   _____

   _____

3. What did Cletus take from the church as a souvenir?

   _____

4. After leaving the Spiritualist church, Ob drove right past the capitol. Then, what did he do?

   _____

   _____

5. Why did Ob go to the capitol after all?

   _____

   _____

6. Summer said Ob was really gentle with her and Cletus at the capitol. In what ways did Ob show his gentleness?

   _____

   _____

7. After the trip, why did Ob ask Cletus to spend the night at the trailer?

   _____

   _____

8. Something flew over Summer's head when she got home from the trip. What was it?

   _____

9. Of what did it remind her, and why did Summer begin to cry when this happened?

   _____

   _____

10. At the end of the book, Ob, Summer, and Cletus carried the whirligigs outside. Why did they do this? How did they feel at the end of the book? What happened in May's garden? (If you need extra space to answer, please use the back of this paper.)

   _____

   _____

Hobby Fair

Ob created whirligigs he called "mysteries." Cletus collected photographs and brochures. Summer liked to write. May enjoyed gardening. What are your hobbies or interests? Learning about someone else's hobby gives you a better understanding of that person. A Hobby Fair is an opportunity for you and your classmates to share each other's passions.

Help provide information to others about your hobby and think about the answers to the questions below (try to include this information in your presentation).

- What is your hobby or interest?
- How long have you had it?
- What made you interested in it?
- Did or do you have to take a class to learn how to do your hobby?
- Is it expensive?
- Who helps you with your hobby?
- How much time do you spend working on your hobby?
- What has your hobby taught you?
- What enjoyment do you get from it?
- Do you know anyone else who has the same hobby?
- Is there anything special that you want us to know?

You can bring in your hobby to school, or if your hobby can not be moved, bring in a visual display of the hobby. The form below can be cut out and used to identify your project.

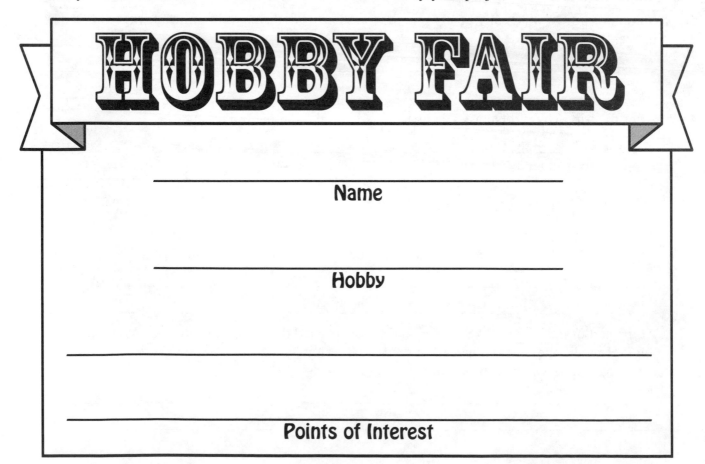

Name

Hobby

Points of Interest

Newscast

Creating and performing a West Virginia Newscast provides pleasurable ways to learn current events; practice map skills and geography; and reinforce skills such as oral language, listening skills, summarizing stories, and restating events—who, what, when, where, why, and how.

Directions

1. Divide the class into an equal number of groups. Each group chooses a newscast name and television channel (for example, Charleston Newsbeat with Channel 5).

2. Assign each student to one of the casting roles below.

   - Anchor Person (This person opens the news with a greeting, gives the world news, and then introduces the other journalists at the appropriate times.)

   - United States News Reporter

   - State News Reporter

   - Local News Reporter

   - On-the-Scene Reporter

   - Interviewer and Interviewee

   - Weatherperson

   - Other roles may also be selected, such as sports reporter or an expert.

3. Groups can research news stories from West Virginia. A great source for current news is *The Charleston Daily Mail*, the Charleston, W.V., afternoon newspaper, located on the Internet at *http://www.dailymail.com.* Have students use the computer and find the weather in Deep Water and other "hot off the press" stories taking place in West Virginia. The paper has local and regional news, weather forecasts, sports, obituaries, and entertainment news. The local reporter may want to include classroom or schoolwide news. Each student is to find a news article and write out a brief summary: who, what, when, where, why, and how. An obituary of May should be included in the broadcast. International news can be gathered from your own larger daily newspaper.

4. Students meet to practice their parts with their news groups.

5. Have students make pictures and logos for their presentations. The weatherperson can have drawings of sunshine or clouds. The world news journalist might want to use a map. The on-the-scene reporter might want to dress as part of the story.

6. The newscast groups take turns performing for each other. (*Note:* Videotape the newscasts for Open House or for the students to watch later. People like seeing themselves on film.)

Psychic Writing Prompts

Summer, Ob, and Cletus were unable to meet with the psychic, Reverend Miriam Young. They were hoping to be able to communicate with May. If the psychic had been alive, perhaps they would have been able to receive a message from May.

Some people believe they can talk with psychics to find out the future. Suppose the Reverend Miriam Young gave you a message. Please write at least one page about what your life will be like. (*Note to the teacher:* Photocopy the prompts below. Cut up the psychic messages and put them into a bowl. Have students randomly select prompts for their writing.)

Writing Prompts

- You will win the lotto. Great news, but everyone wants something from you . . .

- I see a packed suitcase. Soon you will take a trip to an adventurous place . . .

- People are crowded around you. They look to you as a hero/heroine. They lift you in the air and cheer, "Three cheers for . . ."

- As you take a peaceful walk through the countryside, you are approached by two friendly aliens who ask you to go with them . . .

- As you enter the stage, the curtains open, and the crowd applauds . . .

- I see your future clearly—you are the world's greatest flea trainer . . .

- The airplane in which you are flying has to make an emergency landing on a deserted island . . .

- You always said you did not believe in ghosts, but suddenly you have the power to communicate with them . . .

- This is an out-of-this-world experience! NASA has selected you to be the first student to travel to the moon . . .

- Always remember to keep a compass and map with you when you travel . . . I see you become lost while traveling in the Himalayas.

- You will be asked to appear on a famous television program to discuss your latest dinosaur finds . . .

- I see you as a future candidate for president of the United States, but it is uncertain whether or not you win . . .

- After drinking what you thought to be water, a strange feeling comes over you . . . Suddenly, you shrink . . . smaller and smaller . . .

- You will be a very important person. You find a cure for the common cold . . .

- You are in a damp, dark place. Bats are flying around. You are in a cave . . .

- It is 15 degrees below zero. You are getting ready to enter the Iditarod—the annual 300-mile dogsled race . . .

- There are so many stories you will be able to tell about your trips—I see you sailing around the world . . .

- In the future, you have created the greatest game in the world. Everyone wants to buy it and play

The Best Things in Life Are Free

When Summer was living with the Ohio relatives and feeling like an unwanted homework assignment, she received a gift—two people who wanted her and adopted her—May and Ob. All of a sudden, her life was full of love. Summer felt like something wonderful had happened to her. But May was afraid of the fact that being poor was a problem. May worried about not having the money to give Summer all she truly deserved. She wanted to buy Summer big plastic houses with the little round-headed people sitting inside and big baby dolls that wet their diapers. She wanted to dress her in pink and yellow every day and take Summer over to Charleston to the big glass mall and go in the big department store and buy everything in pink and yellow for little girls. But they just did not have the money.

As for Cletus, there was no gift Ob could have given Cletus that would have meant more to him than going to the capitol in Charleston. Aside from the gas to get there, and lunch, the trip was virtually free.

Directions

1. Divide the class into two parts for a debate. One half will take the position that "The Best Things in Life Are Free," and the other half will talk about how "The Best Things in Life Are Not Free." Let the groups meet for ten minutes and formulate their major arguments.

2. The teacher should moderate the event, putting major points made by each side on the board as the sides face off. Try to let as many students as possible participate.

3. When the debate is over, review the points.

4. Vote.

Extension

In their personal response journals or on a separate sheet of paper, tell students they are now free to hold any opinion they wish. Ask students to think about their own lives. Have them think about what they value—what means the most to them. Assign a one-page essay about whether or not they agree that "The Best Things in Life Are Free." Tell them they should give reasons why they think as they do and tell them to support their opinions with examples from their lives.

Any Questions?

When you have finished reading *Missing May*, write possible answers to some of the unanswered questions below on a separate piece of paper. You may choose to work alone or in small groups.

- Who would take care of Summer if Ob died?

- Why didn't Ob want to get out of bed? Why did he stay in his pajamas all day?

- Why did Ob turn the car around and return to Charleston?

- Why didn't they stay overnight in Charleston?

- Why didn't Ob drop off Cletus at his own home after the trip rather than letting him sleep overnight at their trailer?

- Describe Ob, Summer, and Cletus.

- How would the story change if they had met Reverend Miriam B. Young?

- What message would the psychic have given Ob and Summer?

- How did the setting influence the plot of the story?

- What was the significance of water in the story?

- Will Summer become a writer? Why or why not?

- Is it possible for Cletus to grow up and become a legislator for West Virginia and get to work in the State House in Charleston?

- If you had a chance to meet one of the characters, whom would you want to meet and why?

Did you have any questions that were left unanswered? Write some of your questions here and then answer them on the separate sheet of paper.

_____

_____

_____

_____

_____

_____

_____

_____

_____

Book Report Ideas

Book reports come in many shapes and sizes. When you are able to select a type of book report that appeals to you, your imagination can help you create colorful, interesting, and exciting ways to show what you know. When you finish reading *Missing May*, choose one method of reporting on the book. It may be a way your teacher suggests, an idea of your own, or one of the ways mentioned below.

Interview a Character

This can be done alone or with a partner. Choose a character and ask and answer ten relevant questions.

Book Cover

Design a new book cover for the book. Follow the following format: front (book title, author, draw a picture), back (write a summary of the story), inside the right flap (write about an event that took place), and inside the left flap (write about the setting).

Puppet Show

Make two or more puppets and act out a scene from the book.

Build a Mobile

Design your own mobile and include the title, author, characters, symbols, and events as well as information about each of the mobile pieces.

Game Board

This is a group activity for four in which students work together to create a game board. Pertinent information should be included as well as directions and all playing pieces, such as markers and dice. Some examples might be a journey game board or a mysteries game board.

Add a Chapter

In a group of three, write a sequel to the story.

Mural

Design a mural, using magazines, pictures, and other sources, that gives insight to the story.

Point of View

After choosing the role of a character, you are asked to be on a leading talk show. Dress up as the character. The other students will ask you questions about your life and living in Deep Water. Answer the questions from this person's perspective while in front of your class.

Book Critic

Pretend to be two different book critics. First rate the book "Thumbs Up" and give reasons why you liked it. Then rate the book "Thumbs Down" and give reasons why you didn't like it. Focus on the characters and plot.

Movie Poster

Pretend the book was made into a movie. Make a movie poster like the ones in front of theaters to advertise the *Missing May* movie.

Research Ideas

Work individually or with a group to research one of the topics below. Share what you learn with the rest of the class in a report, diorama, demonstration, or any interesting format you choose. Some good Internet sites for researching are Lycos.com, SimonSays.com, and AskJeeves.com.

- **Appalachia**—Did you know that *Missing May* takes place in part of West Virginia called Appalachia because it is part of the Appalachian Mountains? Cynthia Rylant sets many of her stories in this region because she grew up there. Find out about this area.
- **Appalachian Literature**—A great list of Appalachian literature can be found on the Internet at *http://falcon.jmu.edu* and also in your local library. Compare other literature to *Missing May*.
- **Fantasy Literature**—Another item of interest is the number of references the author makes to two particular books of fantasy literature, *Alice's Adventures in Wonderland* by Lewis Carroll and *The Wonderful Wizard of Oz* by Frank Baum. Find out what makes a story a fantasy.
- **Lewis Carroll** (author of *Alice's Adventures in Wonderland*)—Learn about this author.
- **Frank Baum** (author of *The Wonderful Wizard of Oz* and many other books about Oz)—Find out what caused him to want to write.
- **Water Disasters/Food Control**—In the story, you learned some of the horrors of flooding. May had her troubles with this! What steps can be taken to prevent floods?
- **Bats**—Bats got into their trailer. What can you learn about bats?
- **Owls**—Owls are special in this story. Do a report on owl habits.
- **Surrealism**—Cletus claimed surreal was when you stretched out something real until it became distorted. Research the subject of surrealism. Find out about some surreal artists.
- **Renaissance**—What was the Renaissance?
- **Leonardo Da Vinci**—He drew and sculpted and was an architect and scientist. Find out about this "Renaissance man."
- **Benjamin Franklin**—He was a printer, scientist, inventor, writer, and diplomat. Do some research on this "Renaissance man" and report to your class.
- **Suffragist Movement**—Summer is writing a report on Suffragettes for school. Find out about what she is learning.
- **State of West Virginia**—Two Internet sites for data are *http://www.state.wv.us* and *http://www.westvirginia.com*. Where is West Virginia located? What is it like there? What is its history?
- **Charleston, the capital of West Virginia**—Find out how Charleston became the capital of West Virginia.
- **Spiritualist churches**—What is the history of Spiritualism in the United States?
- **Whirligigs**—How are they created and for what are they used?
- **Funerals**—What do funeral services entail? Research funerals in the U.S.

Describe three things that you read about in *Missing May* about which you would like to learn more.

1. _____

2. _____

3. _____

Tribute to May

In Part 1 of the book, Summer and Ob are so full of grief, they can't move forward with living. In Part 2, they pay tribute to May by honoring her life in a way that was meaningful to them.

Now that you have completed reading *Missing May*, you have learned a great deal about her. Make a tribute web to show May's attributes. List her characteristics on each section of the whirligig. Then write a brief tribute to May, using all of the descriptions or attributes you listed on the whirligig. Write at least one paragraph.

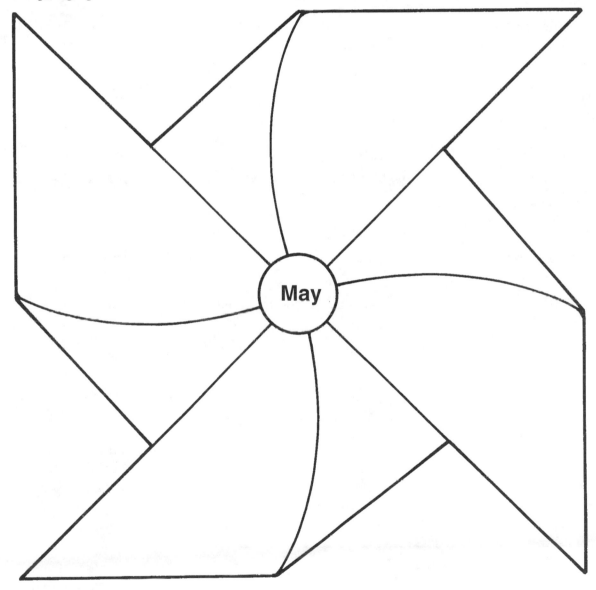

_____

_____

_____

_____

Whirligigs

Whirligigs are usually animals or cartoon characters that spin in the wind. They were used in gardens to scare away birds. An example of a simple whirligig is the pinwheel. You can make pinwheel whirligigs that contain wishes.

Materials (per student)

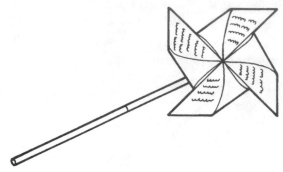

- 9" x 9" (23 cm x 23 cm) white construction paper
- 1 bent-in-half straight pin
- small piece of masking tape
- scissors
- crayons
- 2 straws
- glue

Directions

1. Fold one corner of the construction paper square to another to make a triangle.

2. Fold again to make a smaller triangle.

3. Make sure you have the common fold and fold it upward approximately 1 inch (2.54 cm).

4. Unfold the paper.

5. Write a wish on the inside of one of the folds. Decorate both sides of the paper.

6. Starting at the corner edge of each of the four sides, cut on the fold line until you reach the folded square.

7. Fold over every other piece to the center. The pieces should slightly overlap. Glue one over the other.

8. Pinch together the end of the first straw and place it into the end of the second straw, making one long straw.

9. Push the bent pin into the center of the pinwheel and into the top side of the straw (handle).

10. Tape around the exposed pin.

Take pinwheel whirligigs outside to a garden or windy spot. Let students make their wishes aloud or silently, then let the wind blow their wishes to the sky. If possible, stick pinwheel whirligigs into the classroom garden, as Summer, Ob, and Cletus placed their whirligigs into May's garden in the story.

Extension: If the class did plant a garden, as suggested in Before the Book, gather your harvest and celebrate with a classroom party.

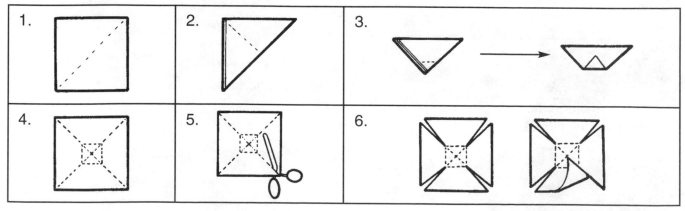

Objective Test and Essay

True or False: Write true or false next to each statement.

1. _____ Summer, Ob, and Cletus live in Deep Water, Ohio.

2. _____ Cletus and Summer are good friends at the start of the book.

3. _____ May would have liked Cletus.

4. _____ Ob made whirligigs that looked like bats and owls.

5. _____ Summer lived in Ohio before living with Ob and May.

Matching: Match the characters to the qualities which identify them.

6. _____ Summer   a. kept an old Chevy in the yard

7. _____ Cletus   b. Small Medium at Large

8. _____ May   c. likes to write

9. _____ Ob   d. observant, odd, collector

10. _____ Rev. Miriam B. Young   e. afraid of water

Sequence: Put these events in order by writing numbers 1 to 10 on the lines. (*Note:* Number 1 is what happened first.)

11. _____ May dies.

12. _____ Summer is passed from relative to relative.

13. _____ Ob, Summer, and Cletus visit Charleston.

14. _____ Cletus introduces his parents to Ob and Summer.

15. _____ An owl flies over Summer's head.

16. _____ May is saved when she is placed in a washtub.

17. _____ Ob, Summer, and Cletus arrive at the church in Putnam County.

18. _____ Ob holds Summer as she cries and cries.

19. _____ Summer comes to live with Ob and May.

20. _____ Cletus arrives with directions to Oz.

Short Answer: In the spaces below, write a brief response to each question.

21. Why did Summer feel like Alice in Wonderland when she arrived to live with May and Ob?

_____

22. Why did Summer compare their trip to the Spiritualist church to the Wizard of Oz?

_____

23. What is the significance of the owl at the end of the story? _____

Essay: Respond to the following questions on the back of this paper. Support your answers with examples from the book.

24. Describe how, and possibly why, Summer and Cletus view the world differently.

25. Why do you think the first section of the book is called "Dark as Night," and the second section called "Set Free"?

Responses

Directions: On a seperate sheet of paper, explain the meaning of each of these quotes or excerpts from *Missing May*.

Chapter 1: Summer says, "I felt like a magical little girl, a chosen little girl, like Alice who has fallen into Wonderland."

Chapter 2: Ob says, "May was right here with us, just now. I swear to God. I felt her, Summer, all up and down me like I'd just poured her in a glass and drunk her."

Chapter 3: Cletus says, "Summer, drop some of them bricks you keep hauling around with you. Life just ain't that heavy."

Chapter 4: Cletus says, "I'm no psychic or nothing. I feel a connection with the spirit world because I've been there."

Chapter 5: Summer said Cletus had a gift—the gift of knowing "when to talk and when not to talk."

Chapter 6: Ob overslept. Summer makes breakfast for him. After giving Summer a long, sad look, Ob pushed his breakfast away and said, "Summer, I don't know that I can do it."

Chapter 7: Ob says to Cletus, "After our little trip, you might be calling yourself a Rent-a-Séance man!"

Chapter 8: Summer says, "It makes me wonder about fear. Whether it all just starts with the people who raise us."

Chapter 9: Ob spoke to Cletus, "Best reading I ever done was in my daddy's old johnnyhouse."

Chapter 9: When the signs on the turnpike started telling us we were coming to Charleston, Cletus became so fidgety that at first I thought we'd better find a filling station, and fast.

Chapter 11: After an owl flew over Summer, she said, "I remembered her then. I remembered May."

Chapter 11: May said to Summer, "I always told Ob he was my moon and sun . . . . you were my shining star."

(*Note to the teacher:* Choose an appropriate number of quotes for your students.)

Conversations

Directions: Work in size-appropriate groups to write or perform one or more of the conversations that might have occurred.

Chapter 1: Ob and May decide to take Summer home to live with them.

Chapter 2: If May's parents were alive when May was a young woman, discuss their conversations as May tells her parents about the man of her dreams.

Chapter 3: Examine the opening conversation Ob had with Cletus when Cletus was snooping around the old Chevy looking for pictures.

Chapter 4: Cletus and Mrs. Davis must have much to talk about as they look through her big box of photos and memorabilia.

Chapter 5: The official funeral for May is not healing for Ob and Summer. Do you remember why it isn't? What are the different conversations that occur at this formal funeral?

Chapter 6: When Summer was in fourth grade, her classmates referred to her as a welfare case. What did they say about her when they were on the playground?

Chapter 7: Suppose Reverend Miriam B. Young was alive. What would the conversation about messages from May be if she spoke with Ob? Summer? Cletus?

Chapter 8: After meeting Ob and Summer, Mr. and Mrs. Underwood (Cletus' parents) talk about their impression of Summer. What do they say?

Chapter 9: Ob says he and Cletus will tell the governor how to "straighten out all this mess." Would they be joking with the governor, or would they be serious? What responses would the governor make?

Chapter 10: If May had a special conversation with Ob and Summer, and she introduced herself to Cletus, what would the conversation be like?

Chapter 11: At the coffee shop where they ate lunch, they eavesdropped on conversations of men and women in their nice suits. What were some of the conversations they might have heard?

Chapter 11: Summer's mother and May converse (or talk) about Summer.

Chapter 12: Ob and Cletus cooked breakfast for Summer and set the table on the morning after their trip.

Chapter 12: There are messages blowing in the wind, setting everything free. What are some of the messages? What might your message be?

Bibliography of Related Resources

Related Books/Articles

Babbitt, Natalie. *Tuck Everlasting*. Farrar Straus & Giroux, 1988.

Bates, Artie Ann. *Ragsale*. Houghton, 1995.

Burch, Robert. *Ida Early Comes over the Mountain*. Viking, 1982.

Byars, Betsy C. *After the Goat Man*. Viking, 1982.

Carson, Jo. *Stories I Ain't Told Nobody Yet*. Orchard, 1989.

Caudill, Rebecca. *A Pocketful of Cricket*. Holt, 1975.

Compton, Joanne. *Jack the Giant Chaser: An Appalachian Tale*. Holiday House, 1993.

Creech, Sharon. *Walk Two Moons*. Harper Trophy, 1996.

Naylor, Phyllis Reynolds. *Shiloh*. Yearling, 1992.

Web Sites

http://cass.etsu.edu/archives/suggread.htm
This East Tennessee State University Appalachia Site has recommended lists of Appalachian fiction and regional nonfiction.

http://www.falcon.edu/ramsey.1/mulappalal.htm
This site by Herb Wilburn has a great description of Appalachia and links to other sites.

http://www.carolhurst.com/subjects/appalachia.html
Carol Hurst's Children's Literature Site has terrific Appalachian information, book suggestions, and synopses.

Other Books by Cynthia Rylant

Appalachia: The Voices of Sleeping Birds. Harcourt Brace, 1991.

Best Wishes. Richard C. Owen, 1992.

A Blue-Eyed Daisy. Bradbury, 1985.

But I'll Be Back Again: An Album. Orchard, 1989.

Children of Christmas: Stories for the Season. Orchard, 1993.

A Couple of Kooks and Other Stories About Love. Orchard, 1990.

The Heavenly Village. Blue Sky, 1999.

A Kindness. Orchard, 1988.

Miss Maggie. Dutton, 1983.

Soda Jerk. Orchard, 1990.

Something Permanent. Harcourt Brace, 1994.

The Van Gogh Café. Scholastic, 1999.

Waiting to Waltz: A Childhood. Simon & Schuster, 1984.

When I Was Young in the Mountains. Dutton, 1992.

Answer Key

Page 10

1. May and Ob were Summer's aunt and uncle who adopted her. May had just died. Summer was the main character.
2. She was passed from family to family from the time her mother died, living with aunts and uncles in Ohio.
3. They fell in love with her and knew she needed a good home. They also saw she was afraid and unhappy where she was.
4. They filled their cupboards with special foods children like, designed a tree house, built a swing for her, and waited with her in the cold for the school bus. Answers will vary.
5. Part of her wanted to go and part of her wanted to stay. She was afraid her home would be gone when she came back.
6. Answers will vary.
7. Ob watched TV and put puzzles together, while Summer read books.
8. Her home and family were swept away and killed in a flash flood when she was nine years old.
9. Cletus was Summer's classmate who wanted to be friends.
10. Summer had been passed around like an "unwanted homework assignment" and had no one to love her. May and Ob wanted a child very badly and loved Summer very much. Their love felt like the best thing that could happen to anyone—like heaven. Answers will vary. Accept appropriate responses.

Pages 13 and 14

Experiment 1: Answers will vary.
Conclusion: Accept appropriate responses.
Experiment 2: Conclusion: The hull-shaped object should float best. Answers may vary.

1. It displaces water. Students answers may be that it is less dense than water or it is lighter than water. Accept appropriate responses.
2. Density = weight/volume. When the volume of an object is increased, its density decreases. Objects less dense than water float. The hollow space in the boat hull decreases its density. Students may say increased air space is the reason. Accept appropriate responses.

Experiment 3: Ice will float in water but sink in alcohol because it is more dense than alcohol.

Page 15

1. $25.31
2. $0.63, $0.50, $1.20
3. $15.96
4. $9.00, Answers will vary.
5. Ellet's store
6. Yes
7. $1.33
8. Ruffles

Page 17

1. He collected pictures because he saw stories in them.
2. His collections came from people he met, magazines, and places he went.
3. Take "something real and stretch it out like a piece of taffy into a thing that's true but distorted."

4. Ob slept in too late, didn't get dressed, and didn't drink his cocoa.
5. He fell in the water and went somewhere with a bright light, where he saw his grandfather and his little dead dog, Cicero.
6. Cletus was the "afterlife antenna." Summer called him that as a joke because antennas help get better TV and radio reception, and Cletus was supposed to help Ob reach further than that.
7. Ob wanted to use Cletus to contact May. He wanted to talk with her.
8. He talked about how she used to rub Ben-Gay on his knee and how she'd open the window and tell Summer she was the best little girl in the world.
9. They were unable to contact May. Summer was disappointed for Ob's sake and because she feared Ob was not coping.
10. Too many people were at the funeral, forcing them to take care of the details of death and practice their manners rather than grieve for May.

Page 20

1. Answers will vary.
2. Answers will vary. Students' details might include feelings, attendees, and purpose.

Page 22

1. Cletus had a flyer from a Spiritualist church which might help Ob talk to May.
2. Ob seemed depressed, did not get out of bed, and was disinterested in whirligigs. Answers will vary.
3. Classmates described Summer as a "welfare case."
4. She did not see herself that way.
5. Ob was not sure he could take care of Summer anymore.
6. He just didn't have it in him.
7. A flyer for the Spiritualist church was hidden there.
8. Ob seemed to need Cletus' help, not Summer's, right now.
9. A Renaissance man is one who could do many things, who had many interests. Cletus wanted to be a "Renaissance man."
10. In *The Wizard of Oz*, Dorothy and other characters traveled to Oz to get help from the Wizard, just as Summer and Ob were traveling to Putnam County to visit the Spiritualist church. Summer wanted Ob to heal. Ob wanted to talk with May.

Page 24

Answers will vary. The following are possible answers:

1. The local observatory offered a "view the stars" night each month for families to stargaze.
2. An article on color blindness discussed testing at local elementary schools to determine student red/green color blindness.
3. This story was about a plant with poisonous bark that made people sick.

Page 25

1. F
2. E
3. B
4. A
5. G

Answer Key

6. D
7. C
8. Answers will vary.
9. Answers will vary.
10. Answers will vary.
11. get acquainted
12. not changing your stance on something
13. feeling uncomfortable
14. happened long ago
15. thinks he or she can do anything
16. naive or young
17. in trouble
18. talks too much
19. not the only person for you
20. straggly looking
21. delicious
22. not letting things bother you

Page 26
1. Cletus' talent was knowing when to talk and when not to talk.
2. Answers will vary.
3. Summer was a talented writer.
4. Ob's gifts were creative whirligigs.
5. May's gift was gardening.
6.–10. Answers will vary.

Page 27
1. Bats got into the trailer.
2. They flapped around in the room, and she heard them.
3. She crushed a bat when she opened a window on which it had roosted. She placed it in a box and tried to feed it and nurse it back to health.
4. Bats came in through the heating ducts.
5. Ob covered the ducts with wire.
6. The real purpose of the trip was to see if the reverend of the Spiritualist church can help Ob contact May.
7. Cletus and Ob were afraid the Underwoods might not understand someone wanting to contact the dead.
8. Ob's reason was to talk to May—maybe to have her back with him, in a sense. Summer's reason was that she didn't want to lose Ob, so she was hoping he would get the answers he needed. Cletus cared about Ob and Summer and wanted to help them. He was also very interested in visiting Charleston. Students' answers may vary. Accept appropriate responses.
9. The directions to Oz were the name and address of Reverend Young and her church in Putnam County.
10. Students' predictions should be supported by facts in the readings up to this point.

Page 31
1. ¹/₂ inch = 3 mi., 0.8 cm = 3 km
2. 4 in., 6.4 cm
3. 5 in., 8.0 cm
4. Charleston
5. southeast
6. 9.23 mi., 14.77 km
7. 68.46 mi., 109.54 km
8. 60, 61, or 64
9. Answers may vary.
10. Travel NW on Hwy 60 until just north of Malden, where you join Hwy 64. Continue NW on 64 until you reach the 214 junction at Charleston. Answers may vary slightly.

Page 32
1.–6. Answers will vary.

Page 33
1. Reverend Young had died.
2. Ob decided to go straight home.
3. Cletus took a flyer from the church.
4. Ob made a U-turn and drove to the capitol.
5. Ob did not want to disappoint the children, who wanted to see the capitol.
6. Ob touched their hair and placed his arms around their shoulders.
7. Ob didn't want to explain the change in their trip plans to Cletus' parents.
8. An owl flew over Summer.
9. The owl reminded her of May, and she became overcome with grief for May.
10. Ob decided his "gigs" needed a new home. The book says the wind set everything free. Students' ideas on this may vary. Theories which can be supported from the text are appropriate.

Page 43
1. False (Deep Water is in West Virginia.)
2. False (Summer does not like Cletus at the start of the book.)
3. True
4. False (Ob's whirligigs do not look like animals.)
5. True
6. c
7. d
8. e
9. a
10. b
11. 4
12. 2
13. 8
14. 6
15. 9
16. 1
17. 7
18. 10
19. 3
20. 5
21. She was so happy to be loved—it was so opposite of what her life had been like before.
22. In both cases, characters took a trip, looking for answers.
23. The owl symbolizes May. Summer remembers May's interest in owls. May is brought to mind with clarity, and Summer realizes she will never be back.
24. Accept appropriate responses. Check for examples that clearly support the writer's opinion.
25. Accept all reasonable and well-supported answers.

Page 44
Accept all reasonable and well-supported answers.

Page 45
Perform the conversations in class. Students listening should respond by asking, "Are the words the students are saying in keeping with the personalities of the characters they are portraying?"